I0503210

The Art of Selling

Learn How To Sell Successfully

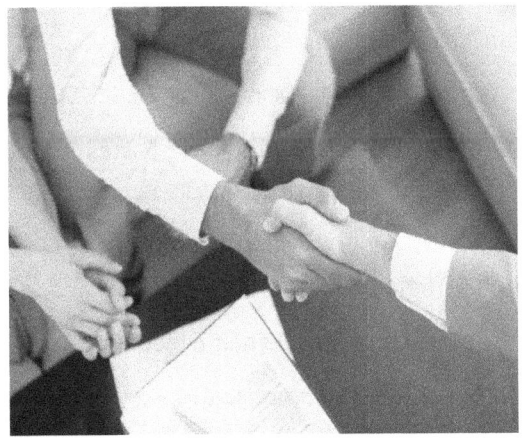

By

Meenakshi Narang

Table of Contents

INTRODUCTION

Selling isn't mere making the prospective buyer buy what he wants or what you may offer. It is also about making the buyer buy your perception about that service or product and start estimating it the way you have projected it.

If you want to be an effective and a reliable salesperson, you must avoid those same old practices and formulate your own game of sales. This book will teach exactly this.

Selling constitutes the essence of all kinds of businesses and every venture involves selling in different ways. This book will throw light on different areas of selling and effective strategies that would help you in boosting sales.

In selling, you also sell your ideas, tangible or intangible products that may not be as simple as they may appear.

Chapter 1- Selling Isn't Mere Selling

Ask yourself a simple yet a vital question – Would you buy a thing that you need on an impulse? I am sure the answer of this question is going to be 'No'. This explains that selling isn't a simplistic game that can be played easily.

Selling is akin to mind game that needs to be first understood and then practiced. It relies on your belief that remains rested in your conscious as well as subconscious mind. For excelling into sales, you ought to grip your thoughts, ideas, gab and the levels of concentration. If we carry some sturdy opinion about the product or the service, and our mind believes in it, our selling power will get auto-empowered. Collect your mind, ponder over its ideas and pour it out in a convincing way. This would set you on the right track and selling won't appear that difficult. It would start coming to you naturally.

The age-old selling ideas have gone redundant for they took consideration of ethical selling. Selling and that in an ethical and valued way would certainly make your buyers believe you every time you will introduce something to them.

Two important ingredients to that would make your sales are the positive attitude and prompt actions. Any delay in thinking or executing your plan would spoil the game. Some of the strategic tips, as told by sales' expert, are –

• There isn't any definite sales strategy that would become a benchmark for all.

• Sales' skills need consistent honing for better results

• The salesperson has to be smarter and rapt than the buyer to make him buy

• Keep on innovating your strategies to not just sell your product but also prove it

• Garner enough willingness, focus and concentration to excel in selling

Ethical Selling: Don't Indulge In Unprincipled Selling

Being a salesperson isn't easy. Even more difficult is to be an ethical salesperson who would sell without losing his or her soul. No one would believe a fake salesperson that puts on the charade of knowing you the moment you are visible. So, stop being like that. Your selling talent has nothing to do with phony affection that often is showered over prospective buyers. The modern buyer is smart and full of knowledge. Even he knows that no business can run without selling. So, instead of using your fake demeanor to sell, resort to some genuine counseling of his needs and sell him your product out of his willingness. Believe in establishing a mutual and cordial relationship with your buyer without imposing yourself.

Here are some ways to be a likable salesperson who believes in sane and rationale selling, unlike those pushy ones who have gone redundant. It is time to change the way things are being sold –

Think Beyond Mere Selling - The buyers are smart enough to gauge your mindset. They can sense if it is tilted towards hardcore selling or genuine for earning their loyalties. You don't have to focus on the word selling. Rather, take yourself as a guide who is going to help people in finding what they precisely need. This way, you would be able to understand the needs of your customers and appeal to their preferences.

Combine Selling with Trust Building - The harder you are trying to sell, farther will your buyers be out of distrust and doubt. Let the whole process of selling and buying be forgotten and lay stress how you can help the customers. Trust me, it is going to show in your body language and you would end up being in trusted books of your buyers. This would consequently help you in recommending your product or service, and you will be believed. The keyword is – 'to be natural and honest'.

Don't Rush - You, as a salesperson, may be a smooth talker. Talks and reasons may be coming to you effortlessly, and you enjoy narrating them. However, selling is not every time ranting about what we know. On meeting a prospective buyer, DO NOT mention your product for first 15 to 20 minutes. If you start chanting about your product, the prospective buyer will shut himself from all sorts of conviction you may present. Ideally, let your customers speak and you listen carefully to know what they want. Your initial silence will go a long way in making the customer getting curious for they would appreciate that you are listening to know their needs.

It's about Expressing and not Impressing- Instead of impressing your customers be expressive and derive same out of them. Do not show them sales jargon where they have to interpret your sales data. Rather, keep your selling approach simple and effortless. Shun the belief that buyers make their mind after watching glossy or flashy presentation. Rather, it makes them distracted from the real profile of the product.

Devise an attractive proposal - There are plenty of products or services out for sale via various platforms. To make your product outstanding, you have to offer what others haven't. If your product is for $200 and you are selling it for $200 only, no rampage would take place. Try selling same product for $50 and some scintillating sale would be conducted. This will add the element of irresistibility to the offer, and a long-term value of the product would get established.

Be Responsible, even after-sale - Most of the salespersons are not gracious in taking after-sales responsibility. This is a significant demarcation between a good and a bad salesperson. In order to carry on ethical selling, one simply cannot remain alienated from what happens to the product or service after the selling. Selling should include a satisfying experience that would come if seller guides the buyers over after-sales issue and helps in resolving same. There should be effective interaction via feedback forms, or tele-calling so that customers can give their feedback or ask for after-sales service.

Vouch for Quality - One simple way to sell without losing your soul is to either deliver quality or return customer's hard earned money. The money-back policy works like wonder as the customer decides to try without any pitfalls for him. A smart seller would not just sell his product. He would rather sell the end results that would endorse his product even further. Buyers will get comfortable and fearless in buying.

Don't Sell Deviously - Selling without any devious methods helps in building long-term bonds. Once buyers get convinced about getting quality products or services, they stop fearing cheating and become loyal customers. Don't just concentrate on 'selling'. Make your selling a worthwhile opportunity that will empower the buyer with not just money but also with a worthwhile product.

For example, you have with you a costly silk wall-panel with intricate design. In a city, it would be priced for more than several thousand dollars. Now you took it to the countryside and sold it for $150 worth of carved wooden chairs. The carpenter may feel happy to get such an exotic silk wall-panel. This deal is completely absurd and futile for the silk wall-panel carries zero value for the carpenter and would remain uselessly hidden in his humble home. As a salesperson, you do not qualify for making an ethical or sensible deal.

Let us rewind the situation and assume that you gave an automated wood peeler worth $100 to that carpenter in exchange of his carved wooden chairs. Now, this would be sensible, and a profiteering deal for the carpenter as that automated peeler will help him in making many more chairs in the future. He would be able to obtain a lot more value of the product you sold him for many years to come.

Chapter 2: How To Be A Successful Salesperson

Selling cannot take place on its own. It always needs a salesperson that would make it a good or a bad. Effective and successful salespersons aren't trained in a day. They hone their skills out of experience and their innate study of customers' tendencies. Here are ten characteristics that would make you a winning salesperson. Find out how many of these do you possess –

➢ **Be Constrictively** - A lot of persistence and determination is needed to be a good salesperson. There would be plenty of instances where you might have to face severe criticism or rejection. During such times, the only determination will keep you afloat. It is not easy to convince someone to buy a thing. It certainly takes a persevering mind set. Just don't give up and you will be an achiever.

➢ **Believe in Goal Setting**– Nothing works without an aim or goal. Expert salespersons devise short as well as long-term goals to meet success. They have clarity over what they want and work strategically towards it. They remain focused towards their goals and work against time to meet them. Ask any good salesperson to show his professional planner and you would see each hour and every day being preplanned.

➢ **Stay Curious** – Good salesperson always has questions running through their minds. They remain aware and ask intelligent questions to their prospective customers. They ask questions to know more and more about their needs in order to fulfill them with their products or services. They are smart enough to endorse their products through their inquisitiveness.

➢ **Listening-** Successful salespersons are good and rapt listeners. They don't believe in using their gab to sell their products. Rather, they gently coax their customers to speak about their needs and then present their products or services in the same light. They first listen carefully and then summarize their selling stance.

➢ **Follow Passion**– Being passionate is the primary requisite for being a successful salesperson. They have to be passionate about their company and the product else their selling will remain hollow and bleak. Good salespersons remain ever in love with their products, and it increases their chances to sell effectively. Their every argument will be convincing enough and will exude their passion.

➢ **Be Liable**– Good salespersons are the responsible bunch of people on whom the companies and entrepreneurs rely. These people take a wholehearted responsibility of the sales results they aspire to generate. Irrespective to all and sundry circumstances they always bear the responsibility of generating maximum sales.

➢ **Active and Agile** - Successful salespersons cannot afford to be laid back else they would miss the leads and lose their contacts. They have to be always in close contact of potential buyers' base even on the personal level. Apart from the sales pitch they remain in touch with the customers to wish them on their birthdays, anniversaries, etc. They follow up promptly and remain in communication via various methods to remain alive in their memories.

➤ **Competitive -**Thin skinned and unsure people cannot, and must not, be part of sales. They have to be confident, persuasive and self-assured as rejection is a common feature here. They must not lose their heart after hearing a 'no'. Rather, they should be able to convert 'no', 'if' or 'but' into affirmation like true challengers.

➤ **Patient and Enduring -** Successful salespersons do not rush into any of the deal as they know how suicidal can it be. They handle their customers patiently and do not throttle them with their non-stop chatter. Impatient salespersons would not do justice to their profile for they would not be able to feel the pulse of the market and the customers.

➤ **Flexible**– Successful salespersons are flexible and adaptive to deal with all kinds of situations and customers. If nothing is working, they quickly alter their strategy and shift the pivot. Selling their products to varied customers would only be possible if they are pliable enough to sing his lyrics in the tunes they understand.

Chapter 3: An Effective Seller is Always Inquisitive

The general notion goes like; customers ask innumerable questions to salespersons to know what are they selling. However, the experts reiterate that salespersons should ask questions in order to first understand the needs of their customers and then to meet their sales target. You need to develop courage and acumen to ask your customers without getting off-track.

Asking Always Helps in Selling

There is nothing offending or probing in asking questions to your customers. Rather, it is appreciable for it leads to better understanding that consequently brings in customers' satisfaction. Varied questions bridge the gap between buyer and seller and solidify their mutual trust. There is also an element of personal bonding that gets developed for a brighter association. Asking also helps by –

✓ Uncovering painful points of customers for better negotiation

✓ Initiating effective closure of sales

✓ Confirming if prospect is genuinely interested in sales' lead

✓ Finding the pulse of the customer

✓ Fine tuning your sales pitch to make it customer-centric

✓ Filtering the customers' information that would help you in selling

What to Ask

The questions listed beneath may not befit every prospect, but would give a fair idea about what to ask, and what not. These questions would also act as prompts and triggers for making prospects come out with their preferences.

Probing Questions – These refer to high order thinking questions that would put prospects on thinking spree. This will have a cascading effect over their issues, fears, pains, needs and requirements that would be addressed by introducing them the right product or service. These questions may be probing but need to be asked for clarity.

Advisory Question – There are times when prospects give vague and confusing information. In such cases, clarifying questions must be asked like – "Can you please elaborate further?"; "Tell something more"; or "What do you want to convey?"

Feedback Questions – It is imperative to ask feedback questions for better insight and further improvement in the sales.

Rapid Questions – Be precise while negotiating. If no outcome is on the anvil, ask for next appointment without any hesitation. This will leave a good impression over the prospect. Ask questions like, "When can we meet next?"; "Would it be possible to meet next week?"; "How about meeting once again for further discussion"?

Committing Questions– If prospect fixes a time, do not hesitate to confirm. Make your prospect commit to you without feeling sheepish. Ask questions like – "Kindly confirm time". You can request prospects to include your call in the schedule so that there can be no amiss.

Sale Questions – After all the ado, don't forget to ask for the sale as an ultimate

question. Ask specific questions like –
"May I have your order please?"; or "Can I
expect a good business with you?"

Recommendation Questions – Referral
questions carry potential of fetching you
further business via interpersonal
networking. These questions have to be
posed with confidence and élan. Ask
questions like – "Would you please refer
someone from your professional circle?"

Chapter 4: Don't Commit These Mistakes To Be A Successful Salesman

Here is a well-researched list of 10 biggest mistakes that are the common pitfalls entrapping salespersons and the way to avoid them:

1. Mindless Blabbering

Most of the salespersons commit the mistake of talking more than they ought to listen. There is no point talking endlessly in front of the prospects and giving them no chance to state their requirements. Ideally, the prospect should be doing nearly 70 percent of the talking. Avoid this by being a patient listener as it will help in gathering the lot of information not just by listening to prospects' words, but also through his body language.

2. **Vague Presumption**

There is no room for vague assumptions in the sales business. Either you know what prospect wants or you don't. Making assumptions can be harmful to they might misfire. You need to understand your prospect, his business needs and then make an offer. Avoid this by being a patient listener and taking a note of every point that prospect brings up.

3. **Being Apologetic or Defensive**

Many salespersons become defensive when confronted by prospects, especially over price issues. Getting defensive and becoming apologetic shows your weakness and would affect the sales' pitch. The prospect will instantly capture your defensiveness through your body language and speech. Such situations should be handled with confidence and promptness. Do not jump to cut the rates simply on mere mention by the prospect. Avoid this by stating USP of your products or services that would justify your price bracket.

4. Failing to make prospect comfortable

Knowing about the budget of the prospect can give you a vital insight. Usually, salespersons do not work towards this. Knowing this area would help them in grabbing the deal easily. Avoid this mistake by asking relevant questions that would make prospect open up and reveal his requirements and the budget threshold he is considering.

5. Unnecessary Follow-Up

The excessive follow-up, on a phone or in person, can irk the prospect and reverse the impact. Too much of chasing of the prospective client appears to be a stubborn behavior that sometimes is taken in a bad taste. Avoid this by making your follow up brief yet effectual. Gather enough information and work over it by staying in the background. Call up only when needed without sounding pesky.

6. Ignoring Affinity-building

Being a salesperson requires social skill and establishing of a rapport that helps in reaping the benefits later. It would be wrong to start discussing sale too early or late. Rather, build an understanding first and then steer towards sales. The absence of mental connection between buyer and seller will be first felt by your prospect only, making him reserved in his demeanor. Avoid this by establishing a mental compatibility with your prospect so that he reveres and believes whatever you say.

7. Pleading to Sell

This is a pathetic mistake committed by most of the salespersons where they act and sound pleading to sell. They perceive as if they have to beg to the prospect in a do-or-die situation to meet their sales target.

This attitude does more harm than good. Avoid this by sounding professional, who has a potential to find the solution to prospects' needs. This would earn you self-respect making you feel good.

8. Working Haphazardly

Following chaotic work approach does not allow for achieving sales goals. Though it is good to be spontaneous and natural in pursuing your sales lead, being unorganized will make things very jumbled. Avoid this by doing your homework well in advance to have an insight into your prospects' needs, followed by systematic and methodical approach.

9. Behaving like competitors

If you are going to sound and act like your ace competitor, how would your prospect distinguish and take a decision.

Being original and authentic will help you in have a different personality from the rest, and you would grip better over your client. This will also help in surpassing the competition. Avoid this by equipping yourself with convincing facts and figures that would elevate the status of your product, leaving no reason to imitate others.

10. Not Prospecting

Prospecting is an integral part of selling. If this is not being done, a lot is being missed. Many salespersons keep on working over months old clients' list without adding or updating same. This is like taking a circular track and reaching nowhere. Avoid this by prospecting effectively through referrals, social media, friends, colleagues, cold calling, etc, one-to-one interaction, etc.

Chapter 5: Know the Kinds of Objections to Handle Them Effectively

How Customers Veil Their Objections

Interestingly, prospects often hide the truth from salespersons. There are only few people who would straightaway say 'No' to a proposal or come out directly with their objections. Now, onus comes over the salesperson to identify the stealth objections and actual reasons of rejections that have been cooking in the minds of customers.

Once the prospect starts evading meeting you and keeps on giving silly excuses, it is time to realize that objections have started developing. If you have tried to overcome initial hiccups and customer still relentlessly driving you nuts, maybe he isn't telling you the real objection and trying to dissuade you this way. Start reading his mind and body language to gather behavioral and contextual clues.

Contemplating the prospects psychologically, he is shying from sharing with you the real objections for the lack of trust. And may be your products are not being seen in very high regard. Or maybe your selling isn't impactful enough to shatter the barriers. Contemplate various reasons that may be bothering prospect ranging from price to quality. If still nothing can be construed, talk to him directly and be politely firm in asking the reasons of his doubt. Your rapport with your prospect will come handy here. Offer to help him to find the solution by taking him in the confidence so that defenses are relaxed.

Use your acumen to find the cause of the objections. Study the pattern and that may give you some clue. Ask plenty of open-ended questions without forcing, to let him divulge what is going inside his mind. Finding objections would be like a game of cards where you have to read through the expressions expertly and come to a precise explanation.

Customers are in a habit of hiding their real objection. Always ask them many open-ended questions and try to read the customer's facial expressions and body language. Put your queries confidently and ask the customer the tough questions. If you do these three things, finding hidden objections will become much easier for you.

Trounce The Objections

What your prospect may be saying on your face may not be the real objection. Once you have played the scrabble of his excuses, and unlocked the mystery, it is time to overcome them. Here are 12 excellent suggestions that would help you in steering past them for successful closure of your sales deal –

✓   Do not jump to respond right at go. Rather, prod your prospect to talk at length over what is bothering him. Gentle prodding will let you know the prime reason of his objection and complete picture can be addressed, and the pertinent solution can be suggested. While prospect would be talking at length about his issue, you would get enough time to think how to respond.

✓   Don't mention price during early stages of the conversation. This would help in keeping the price related objections at bay. Try to get prospect capture the true worth of the product so that pricing will not bother later. An early mention of price results in loss of grip over prospects' articulation and converts discussion towards negotiation.

✓ One best way to resolve most of the objections is to focus not on the product but its worth. If you want to sell an air-frying appliance, sell the idea of saving health by eating oil-free food. Meeting objections is a clear indication that you haven't projected the USP of product in the right way. Touch down the prospects' needs and goals to articulate them accordingly.

✓ Keep calm and slow down your reactions. Acting in haste or on impulse will not resolve any issue. Do not let your emotions take over your common sense. Invest some quality time and thought to push the sale constructively. Prospect may try to make you jittery, but don't give in to the psychological trap.

✓   Many people take the shield of phony objections to negotiate. Get the right picture and identify what exactly is running through his mind. If negotiations are solicited, then steer your selling strategy accordingly. Find the right motive and address it.

✓   Ask the prospect if resolving an issue will help in taking things further or not. This will help you in checking the authenticity of prospect's intention to remain involved in the discussion. If objections are genuine and addressable, alter the package to bridge the gap.

✓   If the need arises, restructure the deal and offer what prospect wants. Subtract or substitute value to meet the mutual objectives midway. However, do not compromise over the quality else your reputation may suffer.

✓   Shoot some intelligent questions that would put the prospect on rethinking mode. Project your product or service smartly to let the prospect think what he may be missing.

✓   Turn the table by arguing from buyer's point of view. If quality is the issue, reiterate the point of quality was stating that's what makes your project stands for. It would be like singing the tunes of your prospect so that he understands it better. Use your expertise to invalidate maneuver objections into your favor.

✓   Evoke emotions and empathy to stir prospect's response. This would work where quality is in question. Making statements like – "We compete for quality and not price" would place you in the elite bracket.

✓ Extend reassurance to the prospect vouching for your product or service. Furbish reference and testimonials to authenticate your claim and to thaw out objections. If a prospect is haranguing over price, assure him of greater value.

✓ One effective way to deal with objections is to make them taste their medicines. If they are dilly dallying with deals, catch them off guard by saying "Take some time to think and reconsider the offer". Prospect will spin his head to realize that a salesperson is asking him to take some time. This will convince him of your confidence. Point out all those things that he may be missing by rejecting the offer.

Chapter 6: Closing The Deal Successfully

The closure should come effortlessly without any tug-of-the-war between you and prospect. After the rigorous pre-sales process, closing of deal deserves to be little lenient according to the set standard. Closure can oscillate towards success as well as the failure, depending the way the whole deal has been settled.

Mastering closure of deals will resolve many hiccups and take advantage of an opportunity.

To master the closing of the sale,

❖   Strategically deal with objections cutting across all the negative tactics and learn how the steer past them victoriously.

❖   Remain attached to the result with a distinctive feeling so that there is no desperation

Having complete control and conviction over your product to have grip over your prospect at the time of closure.

The process of closure cannot be isolated as it gets incepted right through the first and second phase, where trust is established with the prospect and worth of the deal, is shared respectively. The closure comes out to be the last phase that wraps up the whole process. Closure of a sale should -

❖　　Carry no confusion or vagueness

❖　　The terms, rates, clauses and conditions should be articulated clearly

❖　　Prospect's intentions should be recorded and suitable arrangements to be made

When to Close

The sale should be closed not out of persuasion but out of the agreement to meet a decision. If the sale is not coming to a conclusion and problem is still in the lull, a salesperson should take an initiative to ease the whole situation.

Managing Closure out of Rejection

o   If you are closing a deal out of rejection, don't ponder over your failure

o   Keep faith in your sales acumen and talk to yourself positively

o   Don't exaggerate the issue

o   Continue prospecting with better zeal

o   Find a fresh lead and start working over it enthusiastically

How to Close

❖   Close the deal on an encouraging note with due respect to mutual decisions.

❖   If the prospect agrees to deal offered, take them in a guided way to the closure so that they can be relieved.

❖ Keep faith in what you are selling to remain high on commitment and confidence

❖ If closure is accompanying rejection, do not get personal. Keep faith in yourself and carry a positive attitude

❖ Do not leave things unfinished. Take the rejection without aggression, especially if it is in the best interest

❖ Sometimes unfinished deals carry enough scope of revival. Don't stop the ticking of your sales-oriented mind and display persistence

❖ Keep firm belief in your product as it will show your extent of involvement

❖ Hone your negotiation skills to make the closing natural

❖ Close the deal in a confident and a wholehearted manner

Appeal For Direct Close

Appealing for direct close is always advantageous and uncomplicated. It would save you from many hassles and complexities. The direct request would also appeal to prospects and initiate quick wrapping. However, quick closure must not be attempted too early let it may seem abnormal. First establish your trust on the prospect and earn his respect.

Say This While Closing

Sometimes efficiently and effectively presented sales pitch goes wasted simply because the closure was not asked at the first place or not worded properly. As a salesperson, do not take this aspect granted and speak out strategic words. Some of the sentences and phrases are mentioned below that can be contrived suitably -

- "If you will sign the contract by tomorrow, we can get the consignment delivered by the end of the week/month."
- "Should I start devising the contract to get started with the thing?"
- "Would you prefer trying this deal for a week / fortnight / month / quarter?
- "If you are finding it viable, can we initiate the documentation of the contract?"
- "Let's us come to the conclusion and start the paperwork."
- "Are you all set to take things further?"
- "We will book your order on credit so that you can test the grounds."